Celtic

FOLK MAGIC

Publisher
Balthazar Pagani

Graphic design and layout
Bebung

Editing and fact checking Giulia Bilancetti

Vivida

Vivida® is a registered trademark property of White Star s.r.l.

Piazzale Luigi Cadorna, 6
20123 Milano, Italy
www.whitestar.it

Translation: Iceigeo, Milano (Alexa Ahern)
Editing: Phillip Gaskill

ISBN 978-88-544-2184-4
1 2 3 4 5 6 30 29 28 27 26

Printed in China

Giulia Manzi

Celtic

FOLK MAGIC

ILLUSTRATIONS BY
Alice Guidi

Vivida

Contents

Beyond the mist

Sprites, ancient deities, spells that can change the weather, and curses that alter memory—these are just a few of the elements that make the Celtic people so fascinating. Their mysteries have continued to captivate the European imagination, particularly for the traits that set them apart from the Greco-Roman and Hebrew-Christian traditions that shaped Western society.

Rational and materialistic, these dominant schools of thought have often clashed with the Celtic view of life, whose ethics and spirituality were deeply intertwined with a direct, face-to-face relationship with nature.

For the Celts, the material world was inseparable from the *Sídh*, the spiritual realm.

Humanity was seen as part of the Earth, the sacred mother from which all things derive and to which all things return, woven into the vast tapestry of the universe.

Celtic spirituality, then, was less a formal religion and more a system of principles of behavior. At its heart, it can be summed up in one simple idea: recognizing unity in diversity.

This sacred view of life has endured for centuries, breaking through the misty veil of magic that once obscured their customs.

Although hidden from sight and often disguised to survive the passage of time, Celtic traditions have quietly persisted. They live on in folk customs, in the ancient knowledge of medicinal herbs passed down through generations, and in the music and local practices that continue to shape the culture today.

The Celtic preference of orally passing down customs is partly why so much has been lost over time. What we know of them historically today largely comes from the writings of Roman historians, who were fascinated by the Celts' diversity and their unique traditions.

These Indo-European peoples, united not so much by political ties but by shared ethnic, cultural, and linguistic roots, as well as by common spiritual beliefs, have left subtle traces of their presence in the Irish and Breton traditions, which have also preserved some linguistic remnants.

And so, centuries later, we still speak of hidden islands beyond the mist; light candles on the night of Samhain; prepare St. John's water on the eve of June 24; dance around the Maypoles; and wear symbols to protect us from negative energies—carrying forward the legacy of peoples long vanished in time.

Customs, traditions, deities, magical practices, warriors and warrior queens, and an egalitarian way of life that honors the cycle of nature.

The legacy of the Celts continues to resonate with those who listen, revealing the spark of equality in diversity that connects us to the whole.

MAGIC, SPELLS, AND MAGICAL PRACTICES

The ancient Celts possessed a deep knowledge of nature and the spirits that dwelled within it. For them, herbs, plants, trees, and stones were not just physical objects: they embodied the elements and the Great Mother's forces.

This pantheistic worldview was accompanied by a profound reverence for words, song, and poetry. It was through enchanted language that the druids—Celtic priests—shaped the world around them and called upon the powers of nature. Their spells were woven from the properties of herbs, the cycles of solstices and equinoxes, lunar phases, and the art of poetic improvisation.

When we speak of Celtic magic, it's essential to remember that the context in which these practices developed is vastly different from our own. It was a world in which spirit and matter were equally real, and the power of poetry and enchantment could move mountains.

Celtic cushions

Celtic magic was deeply rooted in the natural world and the gifts it provided. To harness the full potential of herbs, the Celts crafted simple handmade cushions—rectangles of thin cloth filled with freshly gathered plants and leaves, ground into powder in equal measure.

These cushions were placed under the pillow, allowing their benefits to be absorbed while resting. The effects typically lasted between three and seven days, after which the herbs would need to be replaced with fresh ones to maintain their potency.

Depending on the plants used, these cushions served different purposes. Some were designed to amplify occult abilities, offer protection, or even facilitate communication with the dead while sleeping.

For example, the cushion used to ward off nightmares contained equal parts of mistletoe powder, cedar, St. John's wort, and mint—an effective blend to repel the evil spirits that haunted dreams.

Spell of restitution

Either for protection or to achieve a more specific outcome, Celtic cushions and pouches were often used in rituals and spells.

One of the most common spells was intended to send negative energies back to their source or to dispel disturbances of unknown origin. To perform the ritual of restitution, one used a red string and a magic cushion (or protective pouch) filled with specific herbs, such as wormwood, eucalyptus, fumitory, and juniper. The ritual began by tying the red string into a knot at its center while visualizing the negative energies moving away from oneself. The pouch was then tied with the string, creating a necklace-like charm to be worn around the neck. One would sleep with it; the next day, the herbs were emptied from the pouch and burned, along with the string, to complete the ritual.

Celtic pouches

Like talismans, Celtic pouches were spells that were meant to be worn. During their creation, these pouches were energetically "charged," imbuing them with power. Once worn, this energy acted like a magnet for the wearer, continuously benefiting from its influence.

While the construction of these pouches was similar to that of the herbal cushions—a simple piece of cloth sewn together to create a pouch—they were intended to be worn throughout the day. Inside, they contained not only herbs, but also runes, stones, and other elements that enhanced their magical properties. The color of the fabric and the astronomical phase during which the pouch was made also played a role in determining its effectiveness.

These Celtic pouches became so popular that they spread across the Western world, particularly in cultures that embraced esotericism and witchcraft. Even today, various neo-pagan and esoteric subcultures continue to use them as part of their spells.

Spell against ulcers and infections

The spell for treating ulcers and infections invoked the power of Dían Cécht, the medicine god and healer of the sick and wounded. Legends say that he would immerse the bodies of fallen warriors in the Fountain of Health, casting his spell to bring them back to life.

The process followed a similar ritual. While the wounds were being washed and disinfected, the spell caster would hold water in the palm of their hand and recite the following words:

"Save those who are sick and wounded, the sores caused by iron, the skin torn by spears, the sudden swellings. Whether it be weakened blood, three broken joints, or three crossed tendons, I smite the sickness, I vanquish the blood and tears of blood. I place all my faith in the remedy that Dían Cécht left to his people, so that every disease may be healed."

Imbas forosna

Imbas forosna is a druidic incantation with various interpretations. Its literal meaning is "illumination in the hands," "science that illuminates," or "inspiration of tradition." Belonging to the group of three spells used to reveal what is hidden, *imbas forosna* was used to uncover the truth about a particular event or the identity of a future king, or to pronounce a prophecy. It was a powerful tool for shedding light on the darkness of the future.

The ritual, which has been passed down to us through Bishop Cormac mac Cuilennáin, involved the sacrifice of a white bull, a red pig, a dog, or a cat. The celebrant would perform the sacrifice and then recite the incantation over a piece of raw meat. After chewing the meat for a long time, the celebrant would invoke the spell once more, using the palms of his hands as a catalyst. He would then place his hands on his cheeks and fall asleep. During his sleep, the prophecy or vision would come to him.

It seems that *imbas forosna* was closely tied to the sacrificed animal, whose spirit would guide the druid in unveiling the future.

Teinm láeda

Teinm láeda can be translated as "breaking the marrow of the essence," "unveiling through song," "splitting the poem," or "illumination of rhymes." This spell was used by druids to uncover hidden knowledge or gain a deeper understanding of a person or object.

To perform the spell, the druid would stand before the person or object in question and begin to improvise a poetic composition. While doing so, the priest would use the *Ogham* sequence on his fingers to guide the composition, simultaneously reciting a poem about the subject to be explored. At the end of the recitation, the druid would place his wand or staff on the person or object, unlocking their past, present, and future.

By harnessing the power of words and inspiration, *teinm láeda* allowed access to true knowledge and revealed the essence of the matter. It was a spell that required years of study, practice, and immense skill to perform correctly.

Glam dicinn

One of the most powerful ancient spells was *glam dicinn*, the "supreme curse," directed at those who violated human or divine law or committed acts of treason or murder. The *glam dicinn* had a dual effect, both magical and social. Three skin rashes would appear on the target, symbolizing shame, offense, and guilt—creating a social stigma that led to their being ostracized from society. Additionally, the offender would die either immediately or within nine days, unless they found a way to redeem themselves.

The death caused by the curse was largely social. Though the *glam dicinn* was intended to channel forces of sickness and death toward the victim, its true power lay in the estrangement from the tribe and abandonment that the offender faced, rather than in any physical magic. It's important to note that anyone struck by the *glam dicinn* could be killed by anyone without facing any repercussions.

Protective amulets

Amulets primarily served a protective role. Sacred symbols were engraved on jewelry made from bone, stone, or metal—such as necklaces, brooches, and clasps—or directly on doorways, fences, and other elements that marked the boundaries of homes.

Some of the best-known sacred symbols are:
- the *triskel:* balance of mind, body, and spirit, healing abilities;
- the *triquetra:* life, death, and reincarnation, associated with maternity;
- the *Celtic knot:* love, eternal union, protection of couples and love;
- the *wuivre:* strength, power, and love.

Even today, the protective power of Celtic symbols can be harnessed by engraving or drawing them on everyday objects. The key is to choose the right symbol for the desired effect. It's recommended to use natural materials—such as stones, which also carry the positive properties of the chosen stone—or noble metals like silver and gold, to enhance the designs and amplify the effects of the symbols.

Cauldron magic

The cauldron, often referred to as the cup or cornucopia of abundance, has always been a symbol deeply linked to female magic. In Celtic mythology, it represented the womb of the Goddess (one example being Cerridwen, a female deity associated with the cauldron), from which life flows, or the heart of Dagda. With the advent of Christianity, the cauldron came to be associated with the Holy Grail, maintaining its role as a vital and magical vessel.

Magical herbs were placed inside the cauldron and boiled for a year and a day. At the end of this period, three blessed drops of wisdom and inspiration would emerge—mirroring the three legs on which the cauldron rested and the three aspects of the Goddess (the Maiden, the Mother, and the Crone).

A symbol of the water element and linked to the cardinal point of the West, the cauldron was—and still can be—used for ritual purposes. By adding salt, sage, or mint to the water inside, it can be used to consecrate or purify objects. The "cleansed" water can also be used to bless sacred spaces and keep negative energies at bay in the home.

PLANTS AND PREPARATIONS

Most Celtic "magic" involved the use of plants, whose esoteric meaning derived directly from the medicinal properties of the plant itself. The strong bond with nature led to the belief that plants, trees, and the elements were true manifestations of divinity, a link between the material world and the divine, which were interconnected.

Many of the plants and trees considered sacred are still very common. The rarity of the plant did not affect its sacred significance. On the contrary, a widespread presence and numerous uses were considered strengths of this "gift" from which humans could greatly benefit.

In addition to a ritual approach to harvesting, we have inherited numerous herbal preparations that have been handed down through popular tradition: poultices, compresses, infusions, decoctions, and oleolites, which can be easily prepared at home to take advantage of the beneficial and magical properties of the herbs they come from.

Oak

Sturdy and majestic, the oak represented strength, power, and endurance. These characteristics made it a symbol of the ability to put down roots and find one's center, but also to resist difficulties.

Inside the oak forests, the druids performed most of their religious rites, including the gathering of the sacred mistletoe that grew on the branches of the trees. It is also said that the druids listened to the rustling of the leaves to interpret divinatory signs.

Oak leaves were also used as ingredients for potions and for protection and purification rituals, as well as being used for their astringent and purifying properties, while their acorns were ground to make bread.

To make an oak decoction, you need to collect some bark, wash it, and put it in a pot with water, bring it to a boil, and filter it. The resulting decoction is used for diarrhea and fever. It can also be used to rub and rinse oily hair, or to wash hands and feet that suffer from excessive sweating.

Ash

The ash tree is one of the five sacred trees of Celtic tradition, which, according to the legend of the druid Fintan mac Bóchra, marked the border of the provinces of Ireland. It was considered a symbol of rebirth, capable of miraculous healing thanks to its fever-reducing, antirheumatic, and diuretic properties.

Traditionally it was believed that its wood could ward off snakes. For this reason and because of its link to Nuada, the great king of the Túatha Dé Dánann associated with clouds and rain, ash was used to make the thrones and staffs of the druids, as well as the ritual spears for young warriors.

By boiling ash bark or leaves in a small pot filled with water until the water starts to change color, you can obtain a decoction that provides relief from cystitis and constipation. It can also be used to wash the face, especially for oily skin.

Hazel

The symbolism of the hazel as a source of knowledge comes from the legend of the spring of Connla: nine hazel trees grew around it, and their fruit nourished five salmon. Whoever ate one of the salmon would receive poetic inspiration and wisdom.

The hazel was also linked to overcoming death and divination. The druids used hazel rods for divination, as well as for dowsing.

Hazel's fruit was considered a lucky charm: the tradition, which later took root in Piedmontese folklore, suggested carrying a handful of hazelnuts in your pocket to bring good luck; finding two hazelnuts stuck together was also a good omen.

A decoction of hazel catkins (pendulous inflorescences full of pollen) can be used to alleviate the symptoms of bronchitis, colds, and coughs. The catkins were also preserved in brine, crumbled to make flour or used in other food preparations as an excellent source of protein.

Apple

A symbol of rebirth and of the legendary island of Avalon, which means "island of apples," it was believed that the apples of Annwn, the Otherworld that could be reached from Avalon itself, had the power to heal any illness. To pass through the veil that separated the mortal world from the fairy world, you had to be holding a branch of an apple tree.

Used in numerous food and alcohol preparations, the apple tree was associated with divine inspiration and poetry; the druids used to carry the Craobh Ciuil (branches of reason), apple tree branches with bronze bells attached, as a symbol of their status.

To prepare an apple liqueur to be used as a digestif, you can make a syrup with 300 g (one and a half cups) of sugar or 150 g (half a cup) of honey in 500 ml (two cups) of water heated over a low flame. When the syrup has cooled, pour it into a hermetically sealed jar with 500 ml (two cups) of 95% alcohol and 130 g (one cup) of apple seeds. After leaving it to rest for a couple of months, shaking the jar from time to time, it can be filtered and bottled.

Alder

The alder tree has always been linked to three fundamental aspects of the Celtic world: clairvoyance, battle, and royalty, due to its association with the god Brân and his legendary exploits. He was considered, before the advent of the god Gwydion, the greatest of kings, a seer and a skilled leader.

Alder wood becomes very hard in water, which is why it was used to build the foundations of stilt houses and bridges. The highest branches were used to make flutes, probably to call storms. Three dyes are still extracted from alder: red from the bark, green from the flowers, and brown from the branches. Its leaves were used to make cloth bags that, when heated, were said to relieve rheumatic and muscular pain.

To treat sore throats, tonsillitis, and pharyngitis, simply boil 30 g (3 tbsp) of alder bark in a liter (four cups) of water for about ten minutes. After leaving to infuse for another ten minutes, filter and gargle the decoction.

Willow

A tree straddling the boundary between land and water, and therefore between life and the world beyond, the willow was associated with the dark goddesses of death and resurrection. Brigit, goddess of spring, carried a willow wand with an acorn at the end to control the weather.

The druids slept under willows to have prophetic dreams, and its leaves were used for the same purpose. They were often worn as amulets to protect from jealousy and keep evil away. Willow wood, used inside and outside the home, protected its occupants from evil influences.

Its analgesic power was often exploited in medicines. In fact, the willow is a natural antirheumatic, fever-reducer, and astringent. One particular use concerns the catkins: left to dry and reduced to powder, they can be used as an analgesic (note: ten catkins have the same effect as two aspirins).

Linden

Imposing and enduring, the linden tree acquired importance over time as a symbol of truth, longevity and sound judgement. Among the Germanic peoples, justice was administered under the linden tree, while for the Scandinavians the protective spirits of the community and the village dwelt in its roots.

The linden was considered the tree of the oracle, which allowed the veil between the worlds to be lifted to gain a glimpse of the future.

The tree was also associated with kindness and hospitality; and weddings and declarations of love were celebrated under the linden tree. Its soft wood was particularly suitable for decorative carving, and its numerous decongestant properties helped to treat sunburn and rashes.

Useful for insomnia and headaches, a cup of tea made of orange and linden blossom will help you to go to sleep more peacefully. To prepare it, simply leave 3 g (1.5 tbsp) of linden blossom and 3 g (1.5 tbsp) of orange leaf to infuse in a cup of boiling water for five minutes. If necessary, you can sweeten it with a little honey.

Elder

Elder trees were a symbol of transformation associated with the realm of the *Sídhe*—which opened near the trees on Midsummer's Eve—and on Samhain, a festival marking the beginning and end of a cycle.

Elder branches were used to make flutes or magic wands. Its leaves were gathered and placed around doors to ward off evil spirits, and the color of the inflorescences was considered a divinatory symbol to foretell a good or bad harvest.

The essence of elder leaves and flowers was used to ward off annoying insects, thus enhancing the plant's protective characteristics.

To prepare an elderberry oleolite, ideal for treating the skin and inflammation and for protecting the home, simply place the freshly picked flowers in a glass jar, cover them with olive oil, and leave them to macerate in the sun for four weeks. Afterwards, it should be pressed and filtered through a paper liquor filter.

Mistletoe

The mistletoe is the most famous plant associated with the Celtic world. It was said to ward off misfortune and disease and bring good luck and serenity. The plant was worshiped as a gift from heaven, and kisses and affection were exchanged under its berries as a good omen for marriage and procreation.

It was believed that the way it "hugged" the bark of trees was not accidental, but was due to the plant's refusal to touch the ground and thus lose its magical properties.

Mistletoe was used to treat numerous ailments, such as arteriosclerosis, gout, and gastrointestinal problems, but it has to be used with great caution, as its berries are toxic.

To prepare mistletoe wine, 30 g (half a cup) of leaves and one liter (four cups) of dry white wine are left to macerate in a hermetically sealed glass jar, shaking occasionally. After a week, it can be filtered and bottled. It is advised to drink two small glasses a day, spaced out between meals, to benefit from its diuretic and antihypertensive properties.

Verbena

Verbena was considered one of the four sacred plants of the Celts, along with mugwort, meadowsweet, and watercress. It was believed to influence dreams, allowing one to remember dreams and prevent nightmares. Druids and priestesses used it to induce premonitory dreams.

Its leaves, burned over a brazier, were used to relax in moments of stress and exhaustion, as well as for fumigations that inspired poetic expression. It was also believed to have magical and aphrodisiac properties.

The decoction obtained from this herbaceous plant was used to treat neuralgia, gallstones, and sunburn, and to stimulate lactation.

Brewing 15 g (6 tbsp) of verbena flowers in half a liter (two cups) of boiling water for ten minutes produces an infusion that can be used to treat sunburn and to relieve tired, puffy eyes.

Meadowsweet

One of the four sacred plants, meadowsweet symbolized love and protection and was associated with truth and wisdom. Known as the queen of the meadows because of its height, which allows it to tower above the surrounding vegetation, meadowsweet's highly fragrant flowers were often used to perfume rooms and drive away bad odors.

It was believed to have a soothing effect on girls, as its extracts were used to treat headaches, which were particularly common during menstruation. The Celts also used the plant as a preservative in the production of mead.

Its strong anti-inflammatory properties meant that it was often used in combination with willow for medicinal purposes—so much so that the drug aspirin was named after the scientific name of this plant (*Spiraea ulmaria*).

Two teaspoons of dried meadowsweet flowers and leaves infused in a cup of boiling water has been shown to soothe digestive problems and mild menstrual pain.

Mugwort

Wreaths of mugwort were placed on the heads of young virgins. The feminine herb par excellence, given to women directly by the mother goddess, it protected against evil and helped travelers, who put the leaves in their shoes to prevent fatigue.

It was gathered at dawn and then one would walk backwards to cover their tracks and avoid being seen by evil forces. Mugwort made childbirth less painful and regulated menstruation, while its vapors, when inhaled, aided dreams and visions. When used in a Celtic pillow, it allowed one to connect with the unconscious and bring to light thoughts that needed to be addressed.

Steeping 2 g (1 tbsp) of mugwort leaves in a cup of boiling water for seven to eight minutes will produce an infusion that will help regulate the menstrual cycle. It is advisable to drink one cup a day, in two separate doses, between meals, starting the treatment four to five days before the onset of menstruation.

Rowan

A protective tree, the rowan was worn as protection against evil spirits, lightning, and witchcraft. A branch placed over the door would ward off unwelcome intruders, while its branches, covered with the skin of a freshly slaughtered bull, were used by druids to summon spirits to answer their questions.

In times of war, druids would light fires with rowan wood and recite spells over them to summon the spirits and invite them to join the battle.

Rowan was also used as a source of food: the dried berries were ground into flour or used to make jams and jellies.

These fruits have great astringent, diuretic, cleansing, and toning properties. Two teaspoons of dried and ground berries infused for five minutes in a cup of boiling water makes a tea that relieves winter sore throats and the symptoms of dysentery.

DIVINATION

From the *Ogham* alphabet and the *Futhark* of the Helvetii to hazel-wood readings and spells that revealed secrets and intentions, the Celtic peoples developed numerous systems of divination whose common feature was their application in rituals and the fact that they had to be performed by priestly figures.

In fact, predicting the future was the prerogative of the druidic caste, more specifically the Gallic *vati* (those who "act" or produce a visible result of their knowledge through prophecy) or the Irish *filíd* ("spell weavers"). The druids interpreted the signs of nature, omens, the positions of the stars, and the weather, as well as the transcriptions of the sacred alphabets and visions in water or fire to allow them to penetrate the veil of time and scrutinize the future.

Ogham: the alphabet of trees

In Celtic society, the druids preserved their culture orally; however, there was also a ritual script reserved for the followers of druidism: *Ogham* (pronounced *Oam*), or the *Ogham* alphabet.

The structure of *Ogham* was based on that of a tree: the trunk (the support, represented by a vertical line), the roots (two strokes extending downward), and the branches (strokes whose angle and position represented the different letters). It was read from the bottom up, following the growth of the trees, so that the message rose from the earth to the sky. Each letter has the name of a tree from which it derives its spiritual meaning.

The *Ogham* were a gift from the god of knowledge and war, Ogma. You can choose an *Ogham* and interpret it according to the symbolism of the tree. For example, the first *Ogham*—*Beth*, the birch tree—invites rebirth, knowledge, and love, so much so that, in some communities, couples would perform the "birch leap" after their wedding to represent the beginning of a new life together.

Runes: the Futhark

Carving symbols on bones, stones, or pieces of wood was a common practice, used both to create protective amulets and to predict the future. The runic system stands out among all methods of divination. It is an alphabet of stylized symbols, each corresponding to a phoneme and a symbolic meaning, which is deeply rooted in everyday life. One of the most famous and ancient alphabets is the *Futhark*, which consists of 24 runes divided into three groups of eight: the *aettir*.

It is said that the god Odin pierced himself with a spear while hanging from Yggdrasill, the cosmic tree. He remained there for nine days and nine nights before gaining the knowledge of the runes.

There are several systems of runic divination, but one of the most common is that of the three Norns, the weaving goddesses of the past, present, and future. It consists of asking a question and then drawing three runes: the first will indicate the cause of the problem, the second will describe the present situation, and the third will give advice on how to resolve the problem quickly and effectively.

Geomancy

Geomancy is one of the oldest divinatory techniques, consisting of reading the Earth itself. In the most archaic forms, a handful of earth was thrown into the air, and the resulting shapes were interpreted according to a group of stylized symbols representing the major situations of life. Geomantic divination could also be performed with elements associated with the Earth or with a strong oracular charge. For example, it was common to use pebbles, small bones, or hazelnuts, the wood of which was believed to have the ability to catalyze divinatory energy. After tossing the oracular instrument into the air, the elements were grouped in fours to create the geomantic figures that, when intertwined, could provide a reading of the future.

Today, geomancy has become mathematical in nature, easily practiced with a sheet of paper, a pencil, a table of geomantic symbols and their meanings, and good concentration.

The ashes of Samhain

On the night before Samhain, now known as All Saints' Day, the spirits of ancestors returned to walk among the living, to protect mortals from the evil spirits passing through from the old to the new year. Samhain also marked the beginning of winter. During this celebration, the druids ordered that all fires be extinguished. Then they would light a new fire, and messengers would carry its red-hot ashes to all the houses in the area, so that each hearth would receive protection from the sacred fire.

On this night, it was possible to perform powerful spells, but the most important prediction consisted of, after the fire had gone out, arranging the ashes in a circle. Inside the circle, a stone was placed for each member of the various families who had participated in the festival. If in the morning a stone had been moved, leaving a visible mark in the ashes, the person who had placed it was destined to die by the end of the year.

SPIRITS AND DEITIES

A world like the Celtic one, where the real and the spiritual merged, is far different from the modern world, where the boundaries between the two dimensions are more defined. It is important to understand that the Celtic tradition placed them on the same level. Celtic spirituality is based on the idea of a single reality, albeit with the ability to manifest itself in many forms.

The complex Celtic pantheon exists within this circular vision, with all its internal contradictions and the difficulties of associating the various divinities with more familiar figures of Greco-Roman origin. The intertwining of Celtic beliefs and deities with history gave rise to semi-legendary figures that often crossed the line between reality and myth.

These divine beings are accompanied by much more unusual figures, such as the mysterious inhabitants of the *Sídh* (the spirit world), also known as the "Fair Folk." Manifestations of nature and the elements are the protagonists of stories that still delight the collective imagination.

Toutatis

Toutatis (or Teutates) was the god of war, fertility, and wealth. As the main Gallic deity, he has often been compared to Mars in the Roman tradition, although Julius Caesar, in his *De Bello Gallico*, identifies him with Mercury as the guide "viarum atque itinerum" (of roads and paths) and calls him "quaestus pecuniae mercaturasque habere vim maximam" (supreme authority in the pursuit of wealth and trade).

As a god of fertility, Toutatis was invoked to protect the fields and the harvest. In fact, it has been speculated that the name "Teutates" (from *theuda*, "land" or "people") could be translated as "God of the Earth." Moreover, this deity could also have represented the "god of the sky," bringer of the rain essential for crops, just like the Roman god Jupiter.

The figure of Toutatis is also known as Albiorix ("king of the world") and Caturix ("king of the battle").

Taranis

Taranis, or "thunderer," is the name given by Marcus Annaeus Lucanus in his poem *Pharsalia* to the Gallic god of thunder, identified by the Romans as Jupiter and by Germanic peoples as Thor. The variants *Taranuo-*, *Taranucno-*, and *Taraino-* have also been found in Celtic inscriptions.

It is probable that he can be identified with the "God of the Wheel," whose iconography shows him standing next to a wheel with a varying number of spokes and holding a scepter, thought to symbolize lightning. It is said that the noise of the wheel of his chariot produced the rumble of thunder that followed the lightning; this legend survived in the Piedmont region, where Taranis was widely worshiped.

Another facet of Taranis was that of Dis Pater, the god of darkness and death. As Jupiter, Taranis was appeased by bloody human sacrifices; as Dis Pater, his victims were burned alive in large wooden vats.

Cernunnos

Worshipped in Gaul, northern Italy, and the southern coast of Britannia, the horned god Cernunnos was the protector of fertility, virility, hunting, war, wilderness, and death. Like Taranis, he was associated with the chthonic figure Dis Pater.

Descriptions of Cernunnos are consistent throughout the Celtic world: he appears as a mature man with a beard and long hair, along with an impressive set of antlers. In his most common depiction, he wears torcs, circular ornaments symbolizing nobility, around his neck, on his wrists, or hanging from his horns. He is depicted with his legs crossed, suggesting a meditative pose or, more likely, the squatting position typical of the Celts during the hunt.

Cernunnos is known in Gallo-Roman religion thanks to the Pillar of the Boatmen, built by Celtic sailors at the beginning of the first century AD, which depicts various Celtic and Roman deities, including Cernunnos.

Lúg

A legendary hero, priestly and military deity, protector of travelers and thieves, guarantor of oaths, truth, and law, Lúg, the god of light and the arts, is a protagonist of Irish ballads and poems.

Tradition identifies him as the heir of Nuada, king of the Túatha Dé Dánann and the first supreme king of Ireland. Lúg possessed one of the four treasures of Ireland, the spear *Sleá Bua*, which guaranteed invincibility to its possessor; and he was the principal architect of the victory of the Túatha Dé Dánann over the Fomóire, "those who come from the sea."

His exploits are recounted in the *Cath Maige Tuired* and the *Lebor Gabála Érenn*. When the Fomóire began to impose heavy taxes on the Túatha Dé Dánann, the alliance between the two groups broke down: Lúg rallied the various peoples of Danu and led them to victory in the Second Battle of Mág Tuired, killing the leader of the enemy, who was his own grandfather, Balor.

Lúg is often depicted with a spear in his hand, blond hair and no beard.

Dagda

In the book of *Lebor Gabála Érenn*, which recounts the cycle of the invasions of Ériu, Dagda, the "good god," was the spiritual father of the Túatha Dé Dánann, as the guardian of druidic wisdom and the owner of the Cauldron of Resurrection (the *Coire an Dagdae*). His club could kill or resurrect whoever it hit, and it was so heavy that it had to be dragged on wheels: the furrow it left in its path was so deep that it could create a border ditch.

Another of his attributes is his ownership of a magic harp, capable of producing wonderful music, but which could only be played when he himself touched the strings.

Married to Mórrígan, he is also known as Eochaid ("he who fights with the badger") and Ollathair ("father of all"), while another of his nicknames is Ruadh Rofhessa, "the red one who knows much," because of his auburn hair.

Although he is said to have reigned over Ériu for eighty years, Dagda is more of a spiritual leader or king of the underworld *Sídh* than a true ruler.

Brigid

Lady of knowledge, goddess of poetry and divination, and also of medicine and metallurgy, Brigid or Brigit was one of the Túatha Dé Dánann.

She is one of the most complex and contradictory figures in the Celtic pantheon. In the *Lebor Gabála Érenn,* she is mentioned as the daughter of Dagda; in the same passage she is also the owner of the oxen Fe and Men, the king of the boars Torc Triath, and the king of the sheep Cirb. Her affinity with the animal world also made her the protector of domesticated animals. In *Cormac's Glossary*, the poet Brigid is accompanied by her sisters Brigid the Healer and Brigid the Blacksmith, suggesting that Brigid may have been a triple deity.

In time, the cult of Brigid spread to Rome, where she was known as Belisama or Brigantia. The Romans also associated her with the goddesses Victoria and Minerva. With the Christianization of the Roman Empire, Brigid was associated with Saint Brigid of Ireland, the wet nurse of Jesus and daughter of the druid Dougal. It is believed that the figure of the Lady of the Lake in the Arthurian cycle was inspired by Brigid.

Túatha Dé Dánann

Legends, stories, and myths about the Túatha Dé Dánann have their roots in ancient times and still survive today in stories about the *Sídhe* and the Fair Folk.

In the *Lebor Gabála Érenn*, the genealogy of this mythical people that invaded Ireland is reported in detail and is intertwined with that of the Fomóire, their main rivals for control of the island. Legend has it that once they arrived in Ériu, the children of the goddess Danu—*Brian*, *Iuchar* and *Iucharba*—burned their ships so as not to be tempted to turn back. They had brought with them four treasures, as legendary as their owners: the *Lia Fail* stone, the *Sleá Bua* spear, the *Claím Solais* sword and the *Coire an Dagdae* cauldron.

The Túatha Dé Dánann spread throughout the island under the guidance of their mythological sovereigns, until they were forced to take refuge in the depths of the earth following their defeat at the hands of the Milesians.

Mórrigan

Mórrígan (or the *Mórrígan*) is the Irish goddess of war who, along with *Badb Chatha* and *Nemain*, is part of the triad of warrior-furies of Túatha Dé Dánann. In the *Lebor Gabála Érenn* and in *Cormac's Glossary*, she is also identified with Anu/Anann, the mother goddess and nurturer of the gods.

A shape-shifting goddess, she takes the form of a crow and hovers over the heads of soldiers about to be killed. She can also appear as an old woman calling warriors to their deaths, or as a woman washing bloody clothes near battlefields.

According to the *Cath Maige Tuired* (part of the Irish mythological cycle), Mórrígan played a crucial role in the battles of Mág Tuired, helping to defeat the Fir Bólg in the first and leading her lover Dagda to victory against the Fomóire in the second.

Mórrígan is also credited with divinatory powers, as evidenced by the two prophecies that conclude the cycle of Mág Tuired battles, in which she foretells a primordial Golden Age and the end of time, and the Dark Age that will follow.

Ankou

Tall, skeletal, and wrapped in a shroud, Ankou is a harbinger of death and the servant of the Black Lady in Breton mythology. His job is to collect souls and take them to the underworld in his chariot, called *karr an Ankoù*, or Ankou's chariot. Anyone who hears its squeaking and screeching noise, caused by the weight of the souls of the deceased, is warned of a death that may affect them or someone in their family.

In the coastal region of Brittany, the cart is replaced by a boat, the *bag noz* (night boat), which carries the souls to the underworld.

In both cases, the Ankou holds a scythe, which, unlike ordinary scythes, has a blade on the outside edge, because Ankou does not bring the scythe to him like reapers do, but instead throws it outward, striking souls from a distance.

It is said that anyone who sees the Ankou will die by the end of the year or be the last person to die in December. That soul is destined to become Ankou's servant and help him in his task.

The inhabitants of Sídh: the "Fair Folk"

While first the Túatha Dé Dánann were forced to retreat to the kingdom of *Sídh* after their defeat at the hands of the Milesians, the advent of Christianity then reduced them to less "dangerous" forms on a doctrinal level, making them lose their importance, until they literally shrank in size.

Fairies, elves, elemental spirits, and gnomes replaced the old gods in dreams, fairy tales, and legends, allowing the pagan beliefs to survive in the stories of the "Fair Folk" (or just "Folk"). The process of overlapping was fueled by the deep-rooted Celtic belief in being part of the whole. The roaring power of nature, expressed in every element, permeated both the invisible creatures of the *Sídh* and human beings. Thus, stories of folklore inherited and passed on the druidic knowledge, and the deities continued to live in the fairy creatures that enrich European folk tales.

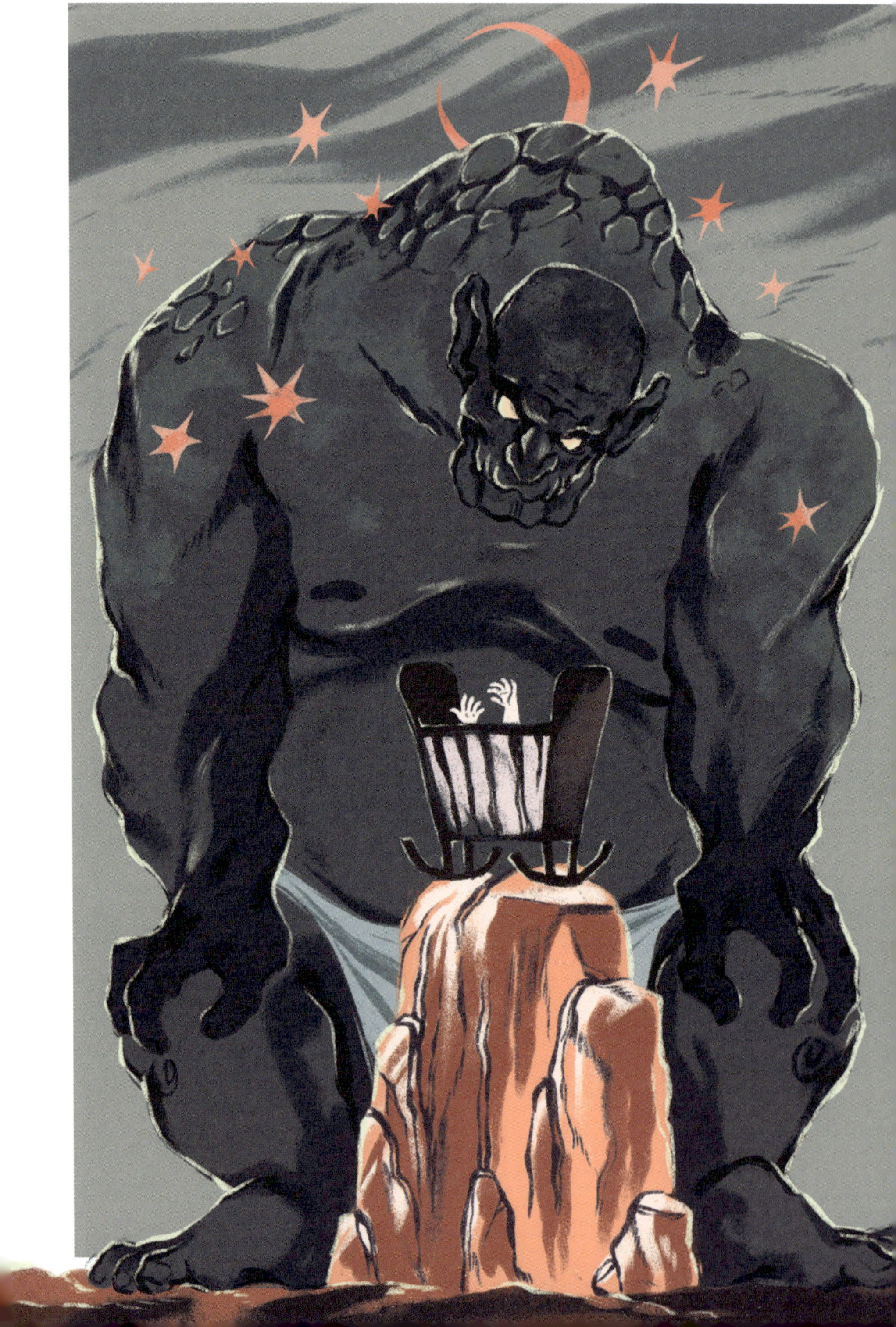

Trolls

Grotesque and hairy, with varying dimensions and characteristics according to the tradition, the troll is a figure of Anglo-Saxon folklore. Often described as an evil giant similar to an ogre, or more rarely as a mischievous humanoid, the troll lives in natural environments and tends to be a nocturnal creature (Scandinavian folklore says that if a troll is struck by the sun's rays, it turns to stone).

Trolls generally live in communities; they tend to be wary of humans, though they are fascinated by them and will often exchange their children or a *changeling* for human babies. Their typical description—clumsy and deformed, with only three or four fingers on each hand, and mammoth in size—identifies the trolls with the Fomóire, the main rivals of the Túatha Dé Dánann. Not for nothing is Balor, Lúg's grandfather, described as being so gigantic that the eyelid of his right eye, which could petrify his enemies, had to be lifted by four men in battle.

Elves

Elves have features that are a cross between gods and humans. They are the *Sídhe* (dwellers of the *Sídh*) who most closely resemble the original divine form of the Túatha Dé Dánann. They took the name Daoine Sídhe when, after being defeated by the Milesians, they sought refuge underground or in the world beyond the mist, a land called *Færie*.

As a folkloric remnant of the people of Danu, they are described as a fairy and semi-divine people of *Annwyn*: tall, beautiful, with a keen and versatile intelligence, as well as fierce fighters. Hidden from the human communities, they occasionally mingled with them and interfered in their affairs. With the advent of Christianity, the elves also saw their role and size diminish. They were reduced to small, mischievous creatures, more akin to goblins, who tended to make livestock sick, and to cause paralysis, insomnia, and mental disorders in most European folklore. Even in Sicily, the presence of elves is documented in connection with the *donas de fuera*, the "women from elsewhere," or fairies.

Green Man

If you pay enough attention while walking through the forest, it is possible to see a human face made of bark and leaves in the trunks of the trees, watching the passersby. This is the Green Man, the guardian spirit of the forest, who protects it and watches over the behavior of visitors. An archetypal figure associated with the cycle of death and rebirth and with nature itself, the Green Man represents the power of natural spirits.

It is not clear whether he represents an ancient god of vegetation or of fertility: the Green Man has been interpreted as one of the representations of Pan, Cernunnos, and Dionysus, but also as the personification of Spring. The fact remains that his image is present in numerous cultures, in which the man transformed into a tree always takes on the role of guardian.

The first representations of the Green Man as a human face made of leaves date back to Roman times; today, the Green Man survives in folklore and in May Day parades under the guise of Jack o' the Green.

Pooka

The pooka, *púca, pwca,* or *puck* is a woodland spirit of British Celtic folklore. Often associated with goblins and hobgoblins, it is a member of the fairy population and, like many of these creatures, lures people into the forest at night with enchanting lights and sounds.

Believed to bring both good and bad luck, the pooka is mischievous, cunning, and a habitual liar. It is usually depicted as a small spirit covered in black or white fur. A shape-shifter, it often takes the form of animals such as horses, goats, cats, dogs, and hares. When it assumes human form, it usually retains some animal features, such as a tail or ears.

The pooka tends to appear on special nights, such as the equinoxes and solstices, at times when the realm of the *Sídh* opens to humans. The pooka is the macabre protagonist of legends in which he rips off people's heads to use them as balls, or kidnaps children and eats them. The most famous representation of the pooka is that of the sprite Puck in *A Midsummer Night's Dream* by William Shakespeare.

Merrow

Fish on the bottom and human on top, merrows are the Scottish equivalent of mermaids and mermen. Much sweeter and kinder than the Greek-Roman sea dwellers, these creatures wear a special headdress, the *druith cohuleen*, which allows them to survive underwater. If they lose it or have it stolen, they cannot return to the sea, which is why merrows often form their own families on land. However, if they were to find their headdress again, they would abandon everything to return to their underwater home forever.

Their pronounced sexual dimorphism—male merrows are deformed, with green hair, red noses, and small eyes; the females, on the other hand, have a delicate and alluring appearance—means that the females often spurn the males of their own species, preferring mortals whom they drag into their home beneath the waves to live outside of earthly time.

The first appearances of mermaids date back to the legends of the bards, who tell of games between merrows and *suire* (sea nymphs), or of the merrow who transformed herself into a harp, the bard's instrument par excellence.

Dullahan

Riding furiously on his chestnut steed, the Dullahan, also known as *Colainn Gan Cheann* or the Headless Horseman, wields a human spine as a whip and carries under his arm his own fearsome head, with sharp teeth and wide-open eyes the color of burning coals. His rotting skin emphasizes his role as a messenger of death. This creature of darkness, whose closest affinity is with hobgoblins, brings tidings of an imminent end to those who cross its path. Those who dare to step outside their door as it passes are covered in blood.

Although the most famous Dullahans in literature and legend are male, there are also female variants of this creature, which is believed to be an incarnation of the Celtic god Crom Dubh, protector of fertility, who carried a bushel of seeds on his back.

In some more recent legends, he drives a sinister chariot, overlapping with the figure of Ankou.

HISTORIC FIGURES

Historical sources mention certain figures who had extraordinary abilities or whose passage left a deep mark on Celtic and European history. From the famous Vercingetorix to the mysterious *bandrui*, this knowledge has been passed down to us thanks to a dense network of texts and documents. Since the Celtic populations followed a rigorous oral tradition in which legends, songs, and myths had the same value as facts, most of these testimonies come from the Roman world.

Eutropius, Tacitus, Julius Caesar, Titus Livius, and Cassius Dio were Roman historians fascinated by the Celtic populations, both for their curious traditions and for the unusual magical powers attributed to the druids. The result is a historical reconstruction in which heroes, warriors, powerful rulers, and priests hold legendary status, and in which real-life figures and social roles of the Celtic world always existed at the intersection of reality and myth.

Boudicca

Boudicca, or Boadicea, was queen of the Iceni, a group of Celts in eastern England. She is immortalized in history and legend as the leader of the greatest anti-Roman revolt in Britain.

According to Tacitus, Boudicca belonged to a noble family and later grew up in a second family where she learned military skills; Cassius Dio describes her as a woman with fierce eyes, tawny hair, and an imposing figure. After the death of her husband, Prasutagus, king of the Iceni, the territory was annexed by the Roman Empire, although the sovereign had named his wife and daughters as his heirs. Publicly humiliated and wounded in body and pride, Boudicca gathered the banners of the Iceni and Trinovantes under her command and declared war on Rome.

It was AD 60–61: the Celtic tribes, incited by the great queen, destroyed three important Roman settlements—Camulodunum (Colchester), Londinium (London), and Verulamium (St. Albans)—until they were defeated at the Battle of Watling Street in the Midlands.

Brennus

The mysterious origins of Brennus, Gallic leader of the Celtic Senones tribe, remain shrouded in mystery, but his name is remembered by Eutropius and Livy for the famous sack of Rome in 390 BC.

After uniting the Senones tribes and conquering the lands between Romagna and Piceno, Brennus began to threaten the Etruscan cities, forcing them to ask for Rome's help. The negotiations between the Gauls and the Roman ambassadors quickly deteriorated, and, after numerous defeats, the Roman army took refuge on the Capitoline Hill while the Gauls sacked the city. Although chronicles do not agree on the reasons why Brennus withdrew his troops to northern Italy—an epidemic, famine, revolts—it is during this period that two events occurred that are more legendary than historical: the episode of the geese of the Capitol; and the intervention of Marcus Furius Camillus, which allowed the reorganization of the legionnaires and the reconquest of the city.

Caratacus

Most Celtic historical figures are associated with the anti-Roman opposition. Caratacus, king of the British Catuvellauni, is no exception.

When Verica, king of the Atrebati, asked the Romans for help against the Catuvellauni, the Emperor Claudius took the opportunity to invade Britannia. It was the year AD 43: Caratacus, together with his brother, faced the Roman legions, but defeats at the Medway and the Thames forced him to flee to the west of the island, where he managed to persuade the Silures and the Ordovices to join him against the invaders.

Caratacus fought many battles but was finally defeated at Caer Caradoc. On the run, he found refuge with the Brigantes but was betrayed by Queen Cartimandua, who had him imprisoned and handed over to the Romans.

He is often identified with the legendary Caradog, son of Bran the Blessed, or with the British king Arvirargus. In fact, the latter is credited with Caratacus's exploits in Geoffrey of Monmouth's *Historia Regum Britanniae*.

Vercingetorix

Few Celtic warriors are so well known that they have become a part of pop culture. Vercingetorix is one of them. His name, which translates as "the greatest warrior king," is now generally considered an honorary title, but it certainly sums up the Arverni ruler's destiny: under his leadership, numerous Gallic tribes united to fight the invasion of Gaius Julius Caesar. It was Caesar himself who provided the most detailed account of Vercingetorix, describing him in his *De Bello Gallico* as a dangerous and charismatic man, capable of fascinating the masses and using them in war, as well as a skilled military strategist.

For four years, Vercingetorix managed to keep Caesar's troops at bay, scorching the earth around them. The Battle of Gergovia was the pinnacle of his glory, when he managed to force the Romans to retreat.

He was finally defeated at Alesia by Caesar himself and brought back to Rome as a trophy. He would be celebrated centuries later by the French historian Ernest Lavisse as "the first hero of our history."

Conan Meriadoc

While we have historical evidence of some Celtic leaders, the story of Conan Meriadoc, King of Britannia, has been lost in myth.

He probably lived in the 4th century AD, and his exploits are recounted in the Welsh text *The Dream of Macsen Wledig* and in Geoffrey of Monmouth's *Historia Regum Britanniae*. His biography, somewhere between history and legend, is closely linked to that of his wife, Ursula, daughter of Dionotus of Dumnonia, who was martyred after being captured by the Huns and later canonized as Saint Ursula.

Their union, often celebrated by artists and hagiographers, seems to have been marked by genuine affection. Born a pagan, Conan Meriadoc converted to Christianity in order to fulfill Ursula's wishes and marry her. After the deaths of his wife and father-in-law, he took over the government of Dumnonia and consolidated his power. He died of natural causes around AD 395.

Druids

The druids are shrouded in mystery. Priests, magicians, poets, musicians, and more, the druids were guardians of the spiritual tradition and inherent vision of reality that permeated all of Celtic society.

In the collective imagination, they have the characteristics of sorcerers, a description also found in the *Ulster Cycle*, in which the druids possessed magical powers capable of unleashing storms and evoking the wrath of the gods. A more realistic account is provided by Julius Caesar in *De Bello Gallico*, who describes them as priests, judges, and those responsible for interpreting mysteries, omens, and traditional sacrifices.

The druids described themselves as "serpents," animals that symbolize wisdom and immortality, and they could move away from their *tuath* (tribe) of origin while maintaining their social status and rights. Druidic training, highly specialized and divided into different cultural areas, could take up to twenty years, as it required learning vast knowledge and skills, as well as the entire oral heritage of traditional legends and ballads.

Bandruí

Celtic tradition has repeatedly testified to the presence of priestesses within the druidic class. And although their presence was concealed or downplayed by scholars, the existence of *bandruí*, or "women-druids," is reported in both classical and medieval historical sources.

The existence of exclusively female priestly communities is also proven: Pomponius Mela mentions, in *De Chorographia,* the Gallizenae, inhabitants of the island of Sein in Armorica; in *Annales*, Tacitus describes a clash in which druids and women "resembling furies" incited battle and practiced incantations.

Oracles, visionaries, witches—these women seemed able to peer into the future; understood the use of plants; and commanded the elements. Beyond myth, Celtic goddess priestesses have continued to fascinate the collective imagination. In the Irish epic *Táin Bó Cúailnge*, the story recounts the use of the *imbas forosna* spell by Queen Fidelma, who considered herself a *banfile* (a "woman-poet," the female equivalent of the druidic class of bards).

Senicuda

There are many areas in Italy where the legacy of the druidic and Celtic tradition has survived in folk medicine and magic. In the Aosta Valley there is a particular devotion to the *senicuda*, or "witch," which had both positive and negative meanings for the local people. Although the *senicuda* were mainly female figures, it was not impossible that men could be found among them.

The *senicuda* were endowed with magical powers, which they wielded using a *secret*, a formula used to heal people, dispel fears, and so on. They were healers, usually widows or old women, who were knowledgeable about herbs, their properties, and the right time to gather them, thus earning the reputation of sorceresses. *Secrets* were inherited from older relatives and jealously guarded, since spreading them would compromise their effectiveness. The oral tradition, the ability to impact reality through words, the deep knowledge of plants, and the connection with nature of the *senicuda* are closely linked to the druidic ritualism for which they serve as female heirs.

Alice Guidi

Alice Guidi is an illustrator with a passion for mythology, folklore, and all things ancient or deep-rooted.

Born in May in a little town near Milan, she spent her summers deep in the stunning landscapes and colors of Friuli Venezia Giulia. Growing up, this allowed her to develop an appreciation for both the city, with its chaotic rhythms, and the emotions that Nature sets free.

She has also illustrated *Herbana Witch: A Year in the Forest*.

Giulia Manzi

Giulia Manzi is a philosophy consultant and writer who explores self-understanding through fiction and the languages of imagination. She calls Rome home, a city she believes is the most magical in the world, where she is surrounded by dusty books, a chubby cat, and dried herbs.

In her free time, she writes, reads runes and tarot cards, studies, and does role-playing games.

She has created the *Find Your Magic* tarot deck, the *Rune Magic* deck, and the oracle *Banksy Wisdom: 40 messages through street art.*